INTF

The Mystery of the Cross is the key to the world's salvation. So, as we follow Jesus along the fourteen "stations" of his Way of the Cross, we should expect to encounter the multiple mysteries of the one mystery of the cross that transforms Christian living.

We make the Way of the Cross to enter into this mystery and be transformed.

It is the mystery of Christ's new way of life: the way of grace that is constant dying and rising. We die to what restricts us and live to what opens us. We die to failure and discouragement to live to new hope. We die to the darkened light of culture to live in the life-changing light of Christ. We die to death itself to live for life.

We die to our own way by following Jesus along his Way of the Cross, which leads to death and resurrection.

This is not just a "lenten devotion." It is letting ourselves be confronted—first challenged, then comforted—by the multiple mysteries that are all one in the Mystery of the Cross. At each "station," open your mind to die a little more to what holds you back, and to live a little more in the way that leads to the fullness of life. Those who carry Christ's cross with faith, hope, and love find that it carries them.

Pope Francis wrote: "Jesus' sacrifice on the cross is simply the high point of the way he lived his entire life. Moved by his example, we want to enter fully into the life of our world, sharing the lives of all, listening to their concerns, helping them in all their needs…We are committed to building a new world…not as a burdensome duty, but as the result of a personal decision which brings us joy and gives meaning to our lives" (*Joy of the Gospel*, 269).

This is what it means to walk the Way of the Cross.

The First Station

JESUS IS CONDEMNED TO DEATH

The Mystery of Our New Identity

LEADER The First Station: Jesus is condemned to death.
This is the mystery of our new identity.

We adore you, O Christ, and we bless you.

ALL Because by your holy cross, you have redeemed the world.

READER Pope Francis wrote:

God is not a far-off deity who does not get involved in the world. Rather, Saint Paul tells us, he "became sin." (*Open Mind, Faithful Heart*, p. 27)

Pope Francis is quoting St. Paul in his Second Letter to the Corinthians: "For our sake God made him who knew no sin to be sin, so that in him we might become the righteousness of God."

[A BRIEF MOMENT OF SILENT PRAYER]

LEADER   The mystery of the judgment Pilate pronounced on Jesus is not that Jesus, though innocent, was punished for our sins. It is that God made Jesus, who could not sin, to "be sin" by taking us, with all our sins, into his body. Our sins became the sins of his own flesh. The body Pilate sent to the cross was guilty. When Jesus died in that body, we died "in him." Our sins went down into the grave with Jesus and were annihilated.

We are not just pardoned; we are purified. When we died "in Christ," the person who committed our sins died, and we rose as a "new creation"—Christ's own body on earth—with no record of sin. Each of us says with Saint Paul, "It is no longer I who live; it is Christ who lives in me."

[A BRIEF MOMENT OF SILENT PRAYER]

ALL   Lord, you took on our identity when you were made to "be sin." We took on your identity when we were made to "be divine." Let us live and act always as your body on earth. Amen.

The Second Station

JESUS TAKES UP HIS CROSS

The Mystery of Suffering

Leader   The Second Station: Jesus takes up his cross.
This is the mystery of suffering.

We adore you, O Christ, and we bless you.

All   Because by your holy cross, you have redeemed the world.

Reader   Pope Francis wrote:

If a family is centered on Christ…moments of pain and difficulty will become experiences of union with Jesus on the cross…which transforms difficulties and sufferings into an offering of love. (*The Joy of Love*, 317)

[A BRIEF MOMENT OF SILENT PRAYER]

Leader   Without faith, suffering is just an evil to exterminate. We spontaneously want a savior who will take suffering out of the world by power—by destroying those who cause it.
Jesus' response to suffering is to embrace it. He turns suffering into a blessing by enduring it with love.
We blame God for permitting suffering. But when we do, we are blaming Jesus for accepting the cross.

Jesus never promised to deliver us from suffering; only to "deliver us from evil." He transforms suffering into blessing for those who endure it with faith, with hope, and with love.

Christians try to spare others from suffering. And when we can't, we share it and bear it with them. But we always bear witness to the mystery that suffering is not a curse but a cross. It is a door inviting us into the mystery of love.

[A BRIEF MOMENT OF SILENT PRAYER]

All Lord, you changed curses into crosses. Let us change all crosses into blessings through faith, hope, and love. Amen.

The Third Station

JESUS FALLS FOR THE FIRST TIME

The Mystery of Failure

Leader The Third Station: Jesus falls for the first time.
This is the mystery of failure.

We adore you, O Christ, and we bless you.

All Because by your holy cross, you have redeemed the world.

Reader Pope Francis wrote:

The Christian theology of hope and failure...must begin with the consideration of the passion and death of Jesus. The historical failure of Jesus in his lifetime and the frustration of the hopes of so many people...are the royal road for Christian hope. (*Open Mind, Faithful Heart*, p. 281)

[A BRIEF MOMENT OF SILENT PRAYER]

Leader Jesus is God. But he falls. Do you remember the first time you failed in anything? The first time you fell into sin? Were you tempted to think you were just "bad"? That you were a "failure"? Or did you learn to accept yourself as human?

Jesus falls because he is human. In Jesus, God himself is weak. But Jesus gets up. His response to failure is his victory: he keeps going.

We fail because we are human. But failures don't make us a failure. More important than our failures is how we respond to them.

We are human, but also divine. We don't use our humanity as an excuse for mediocrity. By the power of Jesus within us, we get up and keep going. We are called to "the perfection of love." We reach it by persevering along the stumbling way of the cross.

[A BRIEF MOMENT OF SILENT PRAYER]

All   Lord, when our failures show us we are human, let our perseverance prove that we are also divine. Amen.

The Fourth Station

JESUS MEETS HIS MOTHER

The Mystery of Faith

Leader The Fourth Station: Jesus meets his mother.
This is the mystery of faith.

We adore you, O Christ, and we bless you.

All Because by your holy cross, you have redeemed the world.

Reader Pope Francis wrote:

[As Mary mourned for Jesus], now she grieves for the… crucified poor… Hence we can ask her to enable us to look at this world with eyes of wisdom. (*Laudato Si*, 241)

[A BRIEF MOMENT OF SILENT PRAYER]

Leader When Mary saw her Son staggering under the cross, was she able to change her answer to the angel and say, "Be it done unto him according to your word"? How could she? How could any mother accept as God's will the crucifixion of her son?

But Mary did. She alone, of everyone on earth at that moment, accepted the mystery of the cross as Jesus did. She alone offered his sacrifice with him.

We are called to accept with faith, as she did, the crucifixion of Jesus—and of all the members of his body until the end of time. At every Mass, when the host is lifted up, we join in offering Jesus, ourselves, and every suffering Christian on earth for the redemption of the human race.

Each of us echoes the words of Jesus: "This is my body, given up for you," and—for every member of the human race—"my flesh for the life of the world."

[A BRIEF MOMENT OF SILENT PRAYER]

LEADER Lord, we accept your way of saving the world. Make us one with you in accepting the Father's will—for ourselves and for all those we love. Amen.

The Fifth Station

JESUS IS HELPED BY SIMON OF CYRENE
TO CARRY HIS CROSS

The Mystery of Mission

Leader The Fifth Station: Jesus is helped by Simon of Cyrene
to carry his cross.
This is the mystery of mission.

We adore you, O Christ, and we bless you.

All Because by your holy cross, you have redeemed the world.

Reader Pope Francis wrote:

Fear of the mission…is from the good spirit, especially
if it does not stop there but allows the Lord's strength
to express itself through human weakness. (*Open Mind,
Faithful Heart*, p. 35)

[A BRIEF MOMENT OF SILENT PRAYER]

Leader Jesus was God. But in his humanity God was physically
unable to carry the cross alone. He needed Simon to help
him. Now he needs us.

Simon was no specially chosen saint. He just happened
to be there. Wherever we "happen to be," Jesus needs us
in order to do with us, in us, and through us whatever his
mission calls for then and there.

Correction: Simon was chosen. We all are. Jesus said, "You did not choose me but I chose you. And I appointed you to go and bear fruit, fruit that will last."

God chooses to save the world through human cooperation. As St. Paul reminded us, we are "coworkers" with God in Christ.

That also means, whatever cross we are carrying, Jesus is carrying part of it. Let him.

[A BRIEF MOMENT OF SILENT PRAYER]

All Lord, you needed Simon to help you. And we know you need us. Help us to help you. Amen.

The Sixth Station

VERONICA WIPES THE FACE OF JESUS

The Mystery of Human Expression

Leader The Sixth Station: Veronica wipes the face of Jesus. This is the mystery of human expression.

We adore you, O Christ, and we bless you.

All Because by your holy cross, you have redeemed the world.

Reader Jesus wants us...to touch the suffering flesh of others... Whenever we do...we experience intensely what it is to be part of a people. (*Joy of the Gospel,* 270)

[A BRIEF MOMENT OF SILENT PRAYER]

Leader Veronica gave human expression to her sympathy and love. And in Veronica God himself gave comfort to Jesus.

Everything we do as Christians is divine. Jesus acts with us, in us, and through us, expressing his love, his truth, his self, to everyone we deal with.

Without his human body, Jesus doesn't act on earth. Until Jesus' body was conceived, the Word was not made flesh. Until his body died on the cross, God's love did not redeem the world.

Until we give physical expression to the divine faith, hope, and love in our hearts, God's life in us is invisible. It helps no one but ourselves. What if Mary had cherished Jesus in her womb forever but never given birth? What if Veronica had wept in her heart for Jesus but never showed it?

Our vocation as Christians is to let the love of God take flesh in our physical words and actions.

If we fear to do this, we must overcome our fear by love.

[A BRIEF MOMENT OF SILENT PRAYER]

ALL Lord, help us remove the veil of reserve from our hearts, so that we might dry tears on the face of your body on earth. Amen.

The Seventh Station

JESUS FALLS FOR THE SECOND TIME

The Mystery of Divine Weakness

LEADER The Seventh Station: Jesus falls for the second time. This is the mystery of divine weakness.

We adore you, O Christ, and we bless you.

ALL Because by your holy cross, you have redeemed the world.

READER Pope Francis wrote:

To embrace the cross we need courage, and to remain on it we need constancy… Suffering with Christ and for his sake is what most bolsters our courage. (*Open Mind, Faithful Heart*, p. 62)

[A BRIEF MOMENT OF SILENT PRAYER]

LEADER Even with Simon to help him, Jesus kept falling. He just couldn't carry the cross. His "spirit was willing," but his "flesh was weak." In Jesus, God himself experienced what it is to be weak.

Our first sin may have shocked us. Our repeated sins discourage us. Unless we learn how to deal with weakness.

Weakness is not a problem. Discouragement is. Jesus just never gave up. He carried the cross without looking ahead.

And he never gives up on us. As long as our spirit is willing to carry the cross, we know Jesus is carrying it with us. Then even our weakness is contact with Jesus. If we keep trying, perseverance is the promise of victory.

To hope is to keep trying without the satisfaction of success. If we are united with Jesus, trying itself is success.

[A BRIEF MOMENT OF SILENT PRAYER]

All Lord, you are not "unable to sympathize with our weaknesses," because you "have been tested in every way that we are," without giving up. Let us draw strength from your weakness. Amen.

The Eighth Station

JESUS MEETS THE WOMEN OF JERUSALEM

The Mystery of Freedom from Fear

Leader The Eighth Station: Jesus meets the women of Jerusalem. This is the mystery of freedom from fear.

We adore you, O Christ, and we bless you.

All Because by your holy cross, you have redeemed the world.

Reader Francis wrote, quoting St. Ignatius:

> Experiencing difficulty is nothing exceptional; rather, it is what ordinarily happens in matters of great importance for the divine service and glory. (*Open Mind, Faithful Heart*, p. 66)

[A BRIEF MOMENT OF SILENT PRAYER]

Leader The women crying for Jesus did not understand. They saw nothing but disaster in what was being done to him. Jesus told them, "Do not weep for me, but for yourselves and your children. For the days are surely coming when they will say…to the mountains, 'Fall on us,' and to the hills, 'Cover us.' For if they do these things in the green wood, what will they do in the dry?"

When we reject the nonviolent Messiah and the mystery of salvation through the cross, we eventually have nothing to fall back on but violence. And violence leads to such suffering and destruction that we end up wanting to say to the mountains, "Fall on us," and to the hills, "Cover us."

Human fears lead to destructive human initiatives. But Christians who accept the crucified and risen Messiah fear nothing in this world. We live for the "wedding banquet of the Lamb." Those who kill us just open the door to the party!

Our hope is in hope itself: hope in God, freeing us to love.

[A BRIEF MOMENT OF SILENT PRAYER]

All   Lord, let us fear nothing but separation from you. Strengthen our trust that nothing will ever "separate us from the love of Christ—neither hardship, or distress, or persecution, or famine, or nakedness, or peril, or the sword." Amen.

The Ninth Station

JESUS FALLS FOR THE THIRD TIME

The Mystery of Hope in Hopelessness

Leader The Ninth Station: Jesus falls for the third time. This is the mystery of hope in hopelessness.

We adore you, O Christ, and we bless you.

All Because by your holy cross, you have redeemed the world.

Reader Pope Francis wrote:

Pure hope in God occurs at the moment when, as in the case of Jesus, we are overwhelmed by the sense of having failed completely. (*Open Mind, Faithful Heart*, p. 282)

[A BRIEF MOMENT OF SILENT PRAYER]

Leader When Jesus fell the third time, he didn't know it was the last time. He was too blinded by sweat and blood to see how close he was to the crucifixion site. He may have known for certain he couldn't go any farther.

But he didn't ask if he could make it. It was the Father's will that he should get up. So he did—and found that he was there.

One day we will sin—or fail in some other way—for the last time. We may be convinced we can do no better; that it is useless to keep trying. What we won't know is that this failure is our last; that nothing remains except to make our final surrender to death.

Then we can say, as Paul wrote to Timothy, "I have finished the race, I have kept the faith."

When you are at the end of your strength, don't look ahead. Look up.

[A BRIEF MOMENT OF SILENT PRAYER]

All   Lord, give us strength to give and not to count the cost, to labor and not to look for results, to ask for nothing except to know that we are doing your will. Then let us be with you forever. Amen.

The Tenth Station

JESUS IS STRIPPED OF HIS GARMENTS

The Mystery of Vulnerable Love

Leader   The Tenth Station: Jesus is stripped of his garments. This is the mystery of vulnerable love.

We adore you, O Christ, and we bless you.

All   Because by your holy cross, you have redeemed the world.

Reader   Pope Francis wrote:

Love must be expressed: freely and generously, in words and acts...The right words, spoken at the right time, spoken daily, protect and nurture love. (*The Joy of Love*, 133)

[A BRIEF MOMENT OF SILENT PRAYER]

Leader   When Mary saw her Son stripped before the eyes of the crowd, did she remember Simeon's words to her: "And your own soul a sword shall pierce, that, out of many hearts, thoughts may be revealed"?

Through all his life, Jesus bared his soul to us. When we respond, our own souls are laid bare. This has to be. There is no complete love without nakedness.

But we are afraid to show our emotions, especially to reveal any felt devotion to God. We suppress any expression of faith in public. We keep secret our love for Jesus, who hung naked on the cross to show his love for us—and we hide our love for others, even when they are hanging naked on a cross in front of us.

We need to break through our fear and accept the vulnerability of self-exposure: to give expression to our love for Jesus and for every person we encounter.

Can I accept to be "stripped of my garments" by expressing my love to others?

[A BRIEF MOMENT OF SILENT PRAYER]

All Lord, you held nothing back in revealing your inner self to us. Help us hold nothing back in revealing our true selves to others. Amen.

The Eleventh Station

JESUS IS NAILED TO THE CROSS

The Mystery of Commitment

Leader The Eleventh Station: Jesus is nailed to the cross. This is the mystery of commitment.

We adore you, O Christ, and we bless you.

All Because by your holy cross, you have redeemed the world.

Reader Pope Francis wrote:

Those [united to Jesus]…know that the cross itself is triumph—and therefore their only hope…When they face challenges…they will not come down from the cross… they will continue on with the mission that was given them. (*Open Mind, Faithful Heart*, p. 62)

[A BRIEF MOMENT OF SILENT PRAYER]

Leader It wasn't the nails that kept Jesus on the cross. It was commitment. The nails were just the visible sign of it. When his enemies mocked him, saying "If you are the Son of God, come down from the cross and we will believe," Jesus could have come down. But then, what would he have left us to believe in?

God defines himself 175 times in the Scriptures as "steadfast love." God is love, love that never gives up.

Love is a free choice. Commitment is a moment of free choice that endures.

Jesus did not come down from the cross. United to him, neither will we.

[A BRIEF MOMENT OF SILENT PRAYER]

All   Lord, at baptism each of us pledged our life to you. Since then we have made other commitments in union with you. Give us the "enduring love" to keep those commitments until death. Amen.

The Twelfth Station

JESUS DIES ON THE CROSS

The Mystery of Death

Leader The Twelfth Station: Jesus dies on the cross. This is the mystery of death.

We adore you, O Christ, and we bless you.

All Because by your holy cross, you have redeemed the world.

Reader Pope Francis wrote:

In the cross, we must lose everything in order to gain everything… The invitation is to all or nothing. (*Open Mind, Faithful Heart*, p. 71)

[A BRIEF MOMENT OF SILENT PRAYER]

Leader When Jesus died, he was not passive: he gave himself to the Father: "Jesus, crying with a loud voice, said, 'Father, into your hands I commend my spirit.'"
Christian death is the greatest free act of life. Just to say "Okay" to death in stoic resignation is not a Christian death. We have to die like Jesus, saying, "Yes!"

This is our final and greatest act of love. We know we "love the Lord our God with all our heart, soul, and mind" when we literally accept to leave everything, even life itself, in order to go to God in death. This is the greatest free choice we make in life, and in making it we arrive at "the perfection of love."

Surrender to death is our final purification—not just from sin, but from all attachment to our restricted human way of knowing and judging that keeps us from living totally the divine life of God. Every choice we make in faith is a preparation for Christian death.

[A BRIEF MOMENT OF SILENT PRAYER]

All   Lord, you condensed your whole life into your death. When we die, let us expand our life into the "perfection of love." Amen.

The Thirteenth Station

JESUS IS TAKEN DOWN FROM THE CROSS

The Mystery of Judgment

Leader The Thirteenth Station: Jesus is taken down from the cross. This is the mystery of judgment.

We adore you, O Christ, and we bless you.

All Because by your holy cross, you have redeemed the world.

Reader Pope Francis reminds us how Christians judge success and failure:

If at times our efforts and works seem to fail and produce no fruit, we need to remember that we are followers of Jesus… and his life, humanly speaking, ended in failure, in the failure of the cross. (St. Patrick's Cathedral, Sept. 24, 2015)

[A BRIEF MOMENT OF SILENT PRAYER]

Leader So far as anyone could see, Jesus died a failure. When they took his body down from the cross, nothing had changed in Israel. The poor were still poor, the oppressed were still oppressed, and there was no peace on earth.

And few believed in him. He failed to convert Jerusalem, Capernaum, even the people of his own home town. When he died, only a handful of his followers were with him. Jesus even cried out from the cross, "My God, my God, why have you forsaken me?"

When Jesus died, nothing the people expected of him as Messiah was accomplished. Yet, we know the life of Jesus was the most successful ever lived.

So how do I judge my life? The lives of others? What is the secret of success?

[A BRIEF MOMENT OF SILENT PRAYER]

All   Lord, without your resurrection, your life would have been a failure. Teach us to ask about everything we do: "What value has this for eternity?" Amen.

The Fourteenth Station

JESUS IS LAID IN THE TOMB

The Mystery of Fulfillment

LEADER The Fourteenth Station: Jesus is laid in the tomb.
This is the mystery of fulfillment.

We adore you, O Christ, and we bless you.

ALL Because by your holy cross, you have redeemed the world.

READER Pope Francis wrote:

At the end, we will find ourselves face to face with the infinite beauty of God, and … the mystery of the universe … In the meantime, we come together to take charge of this home which has been entrusted to us. (*Laudato Si'*, 243–244)

[A BRIEF MOMENT OF SILENT PRAYER]

LEADER Jesus' tomb was really a womb: a place from which life would emerge. St. Paul tells us that all who are "buried with him by baptism into death" come out of the water as a "new creation," "born of water and Spirit," empowered to "walk in newness of life" as Christ's body on earth.

Life and death, as people perceive them, are more fiction than fact. We are not truly alive until we know God by the light of faith: "This is eternal life," Jesus said to the Father, "that they may know you, the only true God, and Jesus Christ whom you have sent." And no one is truly dead who is celebrating at "the wedding banquet of the Lamb."

Death is our final birth into Life. That is the mystery of the cross. Our life on earth is a mission to bring the world to new birth, here and now, in the beauty of the kingdom of God.

[A BRIEF MOMENT OF SILENT PRAYER]

All Lord, from out of the tomb, as out of a womb, was born the world's salvation. Let us live to let you give new life to all creation. Amen.

Concluding Prayer

Leader   We have walked the Way of the Cross with Jesus. But it doesn't end here. We ask that what we have seen as we watched Jesus carry his cross, people will see as they watch us carry ours.

Readers   *(If possible, go around the group and have a different reader read each item below.)*

> Lord, let people see, in our liberation from guilt, the mystery of dying and rising in the "Lamb of God."
>
> Lord, let people see, in our transformation of curses into crosses, the mystery of salvation through love.
>
> Lord, let people see, in our response to failure, the mystery of the divine overcoming human failure.
>
> Lord, let people see, in our response to others' pain, the mystery of our faith.
>
> Lord, let people see, in the burdens we shoulder daily, the mystery of our mission.
>
> Lord, let people see, in our self-expression to others, the mystery of Christ in us.
>
> Lord, let people see, in our stumbling perseverance, the mystery of Jesus carrying our cross with us.
>
> Lord, let people see, in our rejection of violence, the mystery of faith without fear.

Lord, let people see, in our refusal to
give up, the mystery of hope.

Lord, let people see, in our self-revelation,
the mystery of vulnerable love.

Lord, let people see, in our "commitment to
commitment," the mystery of God's "steadfast love."

Lord, let people see, in our attitude toward death,
the mystery of total surrender to God.

Lord, let people see, in our judgment of success and
failure, the mystery of the triumph of the cross.

Lord, let people see, in our dedication to
renewal, the mystery of "life to the full."

Leader Finally, Lord, when people see the way we live, let them see your Way of the Cross as the Way of Truth and of Life.

This is the perspective Pope Francis holds up to the church.

Let us go in peace.

also by Fr. David M. Knight

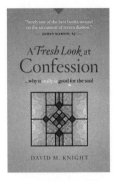

A Fresh Look at Confession
…Why it really is good for the soul

Father Knight speaks clearly about confession and why it is so necessary. His personal experiences take us beyond theory and into the awe-inspiring reality of our redemption in Jesus. Powerful reading for those who struggle with confession or wish to explore this healing and life-giving sacrament.
128 PAGES | $12.95 | 9781585959013

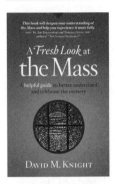

A Fresh Look at the Mass
A Helpful guide to Better Understand and Celebrate the Mystery

Enter into God's awesome mystery by gaining a deeper and more personal understanding of the prayers, gestures, symbols, mysteries, and realities of the Mass. From the Opening Rites, through the Liturgy of the Word and the Eucharist, you'll discover how the Mass brings you to a unique encounter with Jesus. **128 PAGES | $12.95 | 9781627850803**

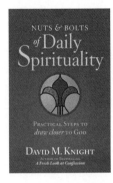

Nuts & Bolts of Daily Spirituality
Practical Steps to Draw Closer to God

Here are practical tips and simple habits anyone can do to enrich their prayer life, get more out of the Mass, deepen relationships, discover the mystical, and get to know God deeply and passionately. Direct and refreshingly simple, these doable solutions can help you grow into "that fullness of life that is the perfection of love."
112 PAGES | $12.95 | 9781585959204

TO ORDER CALL 1-800-321-0411 | **TWENTY-THIRD PUBLICATIONS**
OR VISIT WWW.TWENTYTHIRDPUBLICATIONS.COM
A division of Bayard, Inc.